WORLD'S
SCARIEST
CREATURES
BY JOHN LESLEY
ANGRY
ARTHROPODS
REDBACK
publishing

First published 2025 by
Redback Publishing
Suite 6, 13a Narabang Way,
Belrose NSW 2085
Australia

www.redbackpublishing.com
orders@redbackpublishing.com



ISBN 978-1-761401-70-1

A catalogue record for this book is available from the National Library of Australia

Author: John Lesley
Editors: Lucinda Dodds and Emma Dobinson
Designer: Redback Publishing
Original illustrations © Redback Publishing 2025
Originated by Redback Publishing
Acknowledgements
Abbreviations: l—left, r—right, b—bottom, t—top, c—centre, m—middle
We would like to thank the following for permission to reproduce photographs (images © Shutterstock unless otherwise stated):
pg14br: Tim Bertelink, CC BY-SA 4.0 <https://creativecommons.org/licenses/by-sa/4.0>, via Wikimedia Commons, pg15c: X Prehistorica CM, CC BY 4.0 <https://creativecommons.org/licenses/by/4.0>, via Wikimedia Commons, pg17br: Muséum de Toulouse, CC BY-SA 4.0 <https://creativecommons.org/licenses/by-sa/4.0>, via Wikimedia Commons, pg25lt: Guilherme Ide - AntWiki

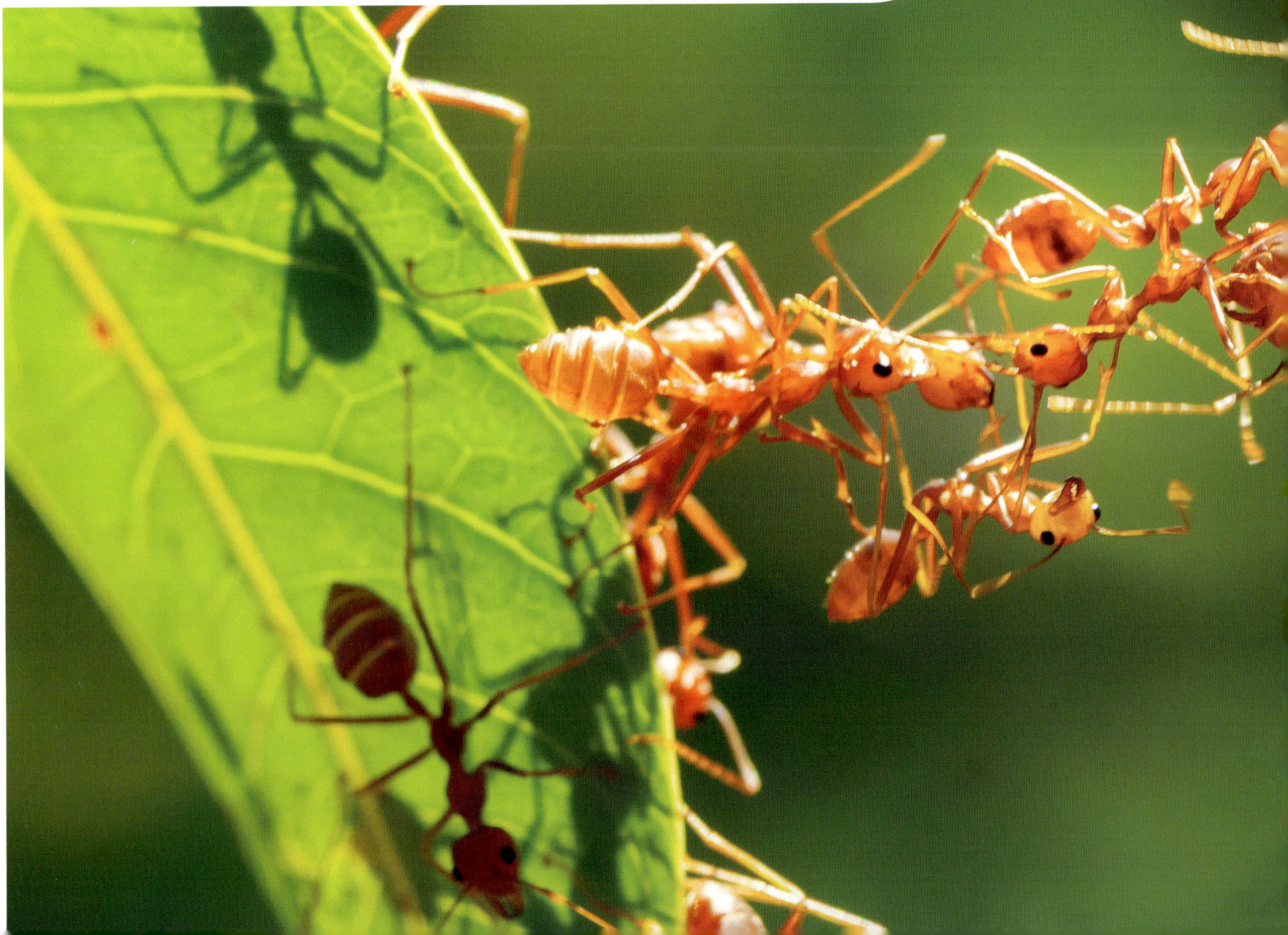

# CONTENTS

# WHAT IS AN ARTHROPOD

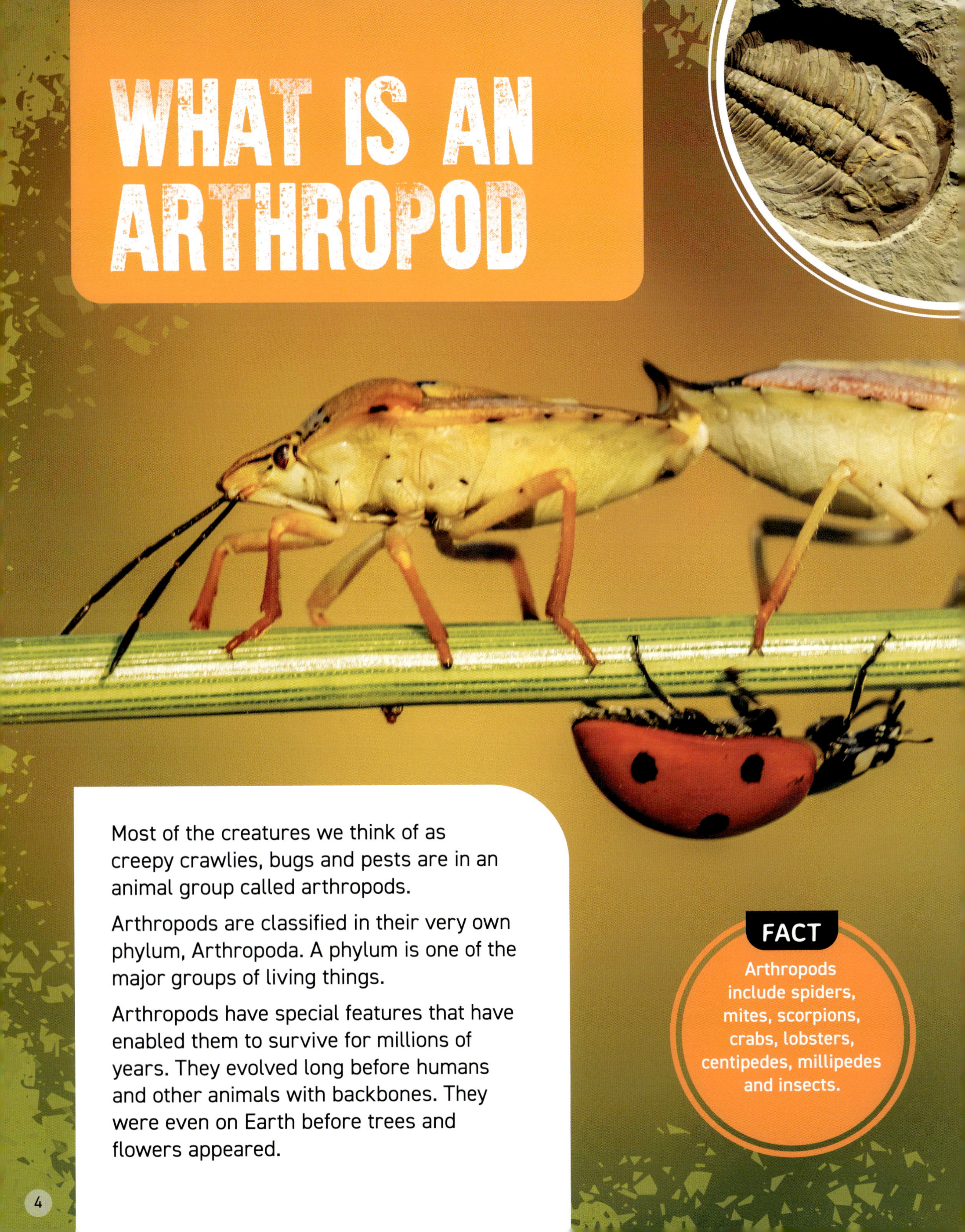

Most of the creatures we think of as creepy crawlies, bugs and pests are in an animal group called arthropods.

Arthropods are classified in their very own phylum, Arthropoda. A phylum is one of the major groups of living things.

Arthropods have special features that have enabled them to survive for millions of years. They evolved long before humans and other animals with backbones. They were even on Earth before trees and flowers appeared.

**FACT**

Arthropods include spiders, mites, scorpions, crabs, lobsters, centipedes, millipedes and insects.

Except for bacteria and viruses, most of all the living things on our planet are arthropods.

# SCORPION

There are more than 2,000 different types of scorpions.

**Scorpions are different from spiders, although they are closely related. Both are called arachnids. They have a scary reputation for inflicting a painful and dangerous sting which may result in death.**

## BODY

Scorpions have eight legs and two large pincers near their head. They use these pincers to grasp prey and hold it still so the tail can move to sting it. The two main parts to the body are a head and thorax at the front, and a long abdomen at the back.

## STINGER

The stinger is at the tip of the scorpion's tail, where it is connected to a sac of poison. Scorpion stings kill thousands of people each year.

## LIFECYCLE

The female gives birth to live baby scorpions. They ride around on her back until their own shells harden.

## FACT FILE

**Length:** from 1 to over 20 centimetres long
**Colour:** black, brown or sandy
**Venomous:** yes
**Life span:** 5-10 years
**People stung and killed each year:** over 2,000

Scorpions have been on Earth for 300-400 million years.

**FACT**

Meerkats eat scorpions by first biting off the stinger.

## HABITAT

Unless you live constantly surrounded with ice and snow, you are likely to encounter a scorpion at some time. They prefer desert habitats, but have been found in all sorts of environments around the world.

## VENOM

Scorpions use their sting and venom to hunt and kill the insects and bugs that they live on. If a human hand or foot gets in their way, they will sting that as well. Not all scorpions are deadly to humans, but their sting can still be painful.

# COCONUT CRAB

*Birgus latro*

**The biggest land crab in the world, and the biggest arthropod, is the coconut crab. It is also called a 'robber crab' because it will sometimes steal food it finds and then run away with it quickly. They have two, very strong pincers.**

**Although they are not aggressive towards humans, their pincers can cut through wood, so keep away!**

## BODY

At over four kilograms in weight, this ten-legged crab is huge. To grow, a coconut crab needs to regularly break out of its thick shell. It takes a few weeks before the new shell is hard enough to protect them from predators.

## LIFECYCLE

The female takes the juveniles to the sea, then returns to her burrow on land. Behaving like their relatives, hermit crabs, the young find a discarded seashell or piece of coconut shell to protect them. Eventually, they grow too big to fit in any shell. They then begin to grow a hard shell, or exoskeleton, of their own which protects their entire body.

**FACT**

Coconut crabs are closely related to the little hermit crabs that some children keep as pets.

## FACT FILE

**Width:** 1 metre, including the legs
**Colour:** mottled brown, blue, orange and red
**Habitat:** islands in the Pacific and Indian Oceans
**Life span:** over 50 years and perhaps even to 100 years
**Scientific name:** *Birgus latro*

Christmas Island in the Indian Ocean has one of the largest populations of coconut crabs.

## WHAT THEY EAT

Coconut crabs are omnivores. They eat fruit, coconuts, seeds and any dead animals they find. Some have been seen hunting birds in trees or small animals on the ground.

## HABITAT

They build a burrow in the ground, but are also often found climbing trees such as the coconut palm. In the places where the coconut crab lives, people sometimes find them in their gardens.

# MURDER WASP

*Vespa mandarinia*

**The Asian giant hornet is the biggest wasp in the world, and has the added name 'murder wasp', for a good reason. As well as a long stinger, they have sharp mandibles or jaws that can cut through flesh.**

## HABITAT

Murder wasps are native to countries of eastern Asia. They gather together in colonies in burrows under the ground.

## FOOD

Murder wasps like to eat bees and can easily eat their way through a whole hive. The wasp has a hard exoskeleton that makes it impossible for the bees to defend themselves by stinging.

## KEEP OUT!

Countries all around the world keep a lookout for any new colonies of murder wasps. If they are accidentally introduced, they could destroy a country's honey industry.

## VENOM

Multiple stings from murder wasps in a colony can kill a person. Each wasp carries a large amount of venom and inserts it with a stinger that is half a centimetre long.

**FACT**

With its wings spread, the murder wasp will fill the palm of a hand.

**FACT FILE**

**Length:** body 5 centimetres long; wingspan 7 centimetres
**Colour:** yellow and black
**Venomous:** yes
**Life span:** queens can live for year, but workers die sooner
**Scientific name:** *Vespa mandarinia*

The pain from a murder wasp sting is much worse than that of a bee.

# CENTIPEDE

**The name centipede literally means having 100 feet. Despite the name, centipedes do not all have 100 feet or legs. They have two legs on each of their body segments.**

**Giant centipedes are called scolopendrid centipedes. They can grow up to thirty centimetres long.**

## HABITAT

The exoskeleton is softer than in some other arthropods, which causes centipedes to seek out damp areas to stop themselves drying out. This is easy in forests or underneath houses, but in deserts they need to burrow under the ground.

## FOOD

Centipedes are carnivores, hunting and eating other small creatures.

## VENOM AND BITING

Centipedes are venomous. They bite and inject venom using special claws near the head. People bitten will have a very sore spot for a number of days.

The number of legs can vary from 30 to over 300.

## FACT FILE

**Length:** ranging from 1 to 30 centimetres
**Colour:** black, brown, orange
**Venomous:** yes
**Habitat:** moist environments
**Life span:** 10 years

## FACT

Millipedes are related to centipedes, but they have four legs on each segment instead of two. Millipedes are herbivores and they do not have venom.

# BIGGEST EVER!

## ARTHROPLEURA

One of the biggest arthropods that has ever existed was a gigantic millipede. It grew to over two metres long, making it the length of a crocodile. Scientists call them *Arthropleura*.

## WHEN?

It lived 300 million years ago, when the temperature on Earth was warmer than today, and the amount of oxygen in the atmosphere was higher. These two conditions allowed this arthropod to grow to a size that would probably not be possible in any of the current habitats available on Earth.

## FOOD

We are not sure what they ate, but it is possible that, unlike modern millipedes, these prehistoric ones were carnivorous hunters.

*Arthropleura* would have weighed about 50 kilograms.

*Arthropleura* lived millions of years before the dinosaurs and long before there were any people.

# GIANT DRAGONFLY

**One of the biggest dragonflies that ever lived was in the genus called *Meganeura*. These enormous, flying hunters flew around the swampy forests of Earth 300 million years ago.**

## WINGSPAN

With a wingspan of over 70 centimetres, they were ferocious hunters of other insects, trapping their prey with the spikes on their legs.

At about 30 centimetres long, *Meganeura* larvae were some of the biggest grubs that have ever existed.

**FACT**

Long before birds or flying dinosaurs evolved, prehistoric dragonflies were the top predators in the air.

# GOLIATH BIRDEATER SPIDER

*Theraphosa blondi*

**Many people have an uncontrollable fear of spiders. This fear is often unnecessary, but when it comes to goliath birdeater spiders, the terror is understandable.**

## HABITAT

This heavy spider is native to the jungles of South America, where it makes a burrow under rocks and dead leaves on the forest floor.

## FOOD

Despite its name, this spider only occasionally hunts and eats birds. It prefers to dine on prey that is slower and easier to catch, like worms and insects.

## VENOM AND BITING

Although these spiders do have venom delivered through long fangs, people bitten rarely get very sick. Some people even keep these spiders as pets.

**The egg sac contains about 100 eggs and is the size of a mandarin.**

## FACT FILE

**Width:** 30 centimetres, including the legs
**Colour:** brown hair
**Venomous:** yes
**Habitat:** South American Rainforests
**Life span:** females may live up to 20 years
**Scientific name:** *Theraphosa blondi*

# MITE

Just because an arthropod is so small that you can only see it under a microscope does not mean that it is harmless. Some of the fiercest arthropods are nearly invisible, breeding in the billions, in water, soil, on plants and on animals.

Mites are related to spiders and have eight tiny legs, and hard jaws that bite. Most of them are almost invisible. Mites bite, spread diseases and can make you sick. They get in your hair, clothes, eyelashes and carpets. If you have an itch right now, it could be because a mite is biting you.

**FACT**

Mites in dust can cause people to develop asthma.

## FACT FILE

**Length:** many are less than 1 millimetre long
**Colour:** mostly brown
**Venomous:** some have venom
**Habitat:** nearly every habitat on Earth
**Life span:** up to a few weeks

Controlling mites is difficult and mainly involves using pesticides.

# SUN SPIDER

**If you see one of these creatures in the wild, you might find it hard to work out if it is a spider or a scorpion. In fact, it is neither. Sun spiders are not spiders at all. They are in their own group of arthropods called solifugids.**

## FOOD

Solifugids hunt any creature small enough for them to catch. They do not use venom, but bite their prey with jaws that can be a third of the sun spider's size.

## THEY ARE FAST

Solifugids are fast runners. They race around at top speed, biting any prey they find, and then they eat it on the way.

## CAMEL SPIDERS

There are a lot of myths around about the size of camel spiders, a close relative of the sun spider. Camel spiders grow to about five centimetres long. While this is big, and they do bite, it does not grow to the huge sizes you will see reported on some Internet sites.

OTHER NAMES:
Sun spiders, camel spiders, wind spiders.

## FACT FILE

**Length:** 5 centimetres
**Colour:** brown, orange
**Venomous:** yes
**Habitat:** arid, warm areas in America, Africa and India
**Common name:** solifugids

## FACT

Sun spiders have jaws that bite their prey into pieces.

# GIANT AMAZON ANT

*Dinoponera*

**The giant Amazon ant is the biggest in the world. Growing to four centimetres long, its bite is horrendously painful and the venom it injects from its sting causes serious health problems for humans.**

## HABITAT

These giant ants build nests on the forest floor. The nest can be a metre deep in the soil, but the number of ants in it is not large. There may be only 100 ants living in one nest, much less than an ordinary ant nest.

## FOOD

The carnivorous worker ants leave the nest to go hunting for small creatures. They leave a scent trail through the forest that other workers can follow. If one finds a good source of food, all the other workers soon gather to take part in the feast as well.

## FACT FILE

**Length:** 4 centimetres
**Colour:** grey-brown, black
**Venomous:** yes
**Habitat:** forests of South America
**Life span:** perhaps over a year
**Scientific name:** *Dinoponera*

## FACT

Ants hold prey with their mandibles then sting it with a stinger located at the other end of their body.

# BEE SWARMS

Bees make honey for us, but they are under threat around the world from climate change, disease, mites and overuse of pesticides. Despite this, if a swarm of bees ends up in a tree near your window, or even in the roof of your house, you want them gone by any means possible.

A bee swarm is dangerous to be near. They are looking for somewhere to set up a new hive, and if you get in the way then you will be stung.

Somewhere in the noisy swarm there will be a queen bee. Beekeepers who know how to control a swarm will look for the queen. Once she is moved, all the workers in the swarm will follow her.

**FACT**

Leave the bees alone and calmly move away so you don't disturb the swarm.

A bee swarm can include over 30,000 bees.

# ARTHROPOD BASIC FACTS

## EXOSKELETONS

Arthropods have hard exoskeletons that provide protection and support. The shells of lobsters and the outer armour on ants are examples of exoskeletons.

## SEGMENTED BODIES

Arthropods have bodies that are divided into segments. This allows them to bend and move easily.

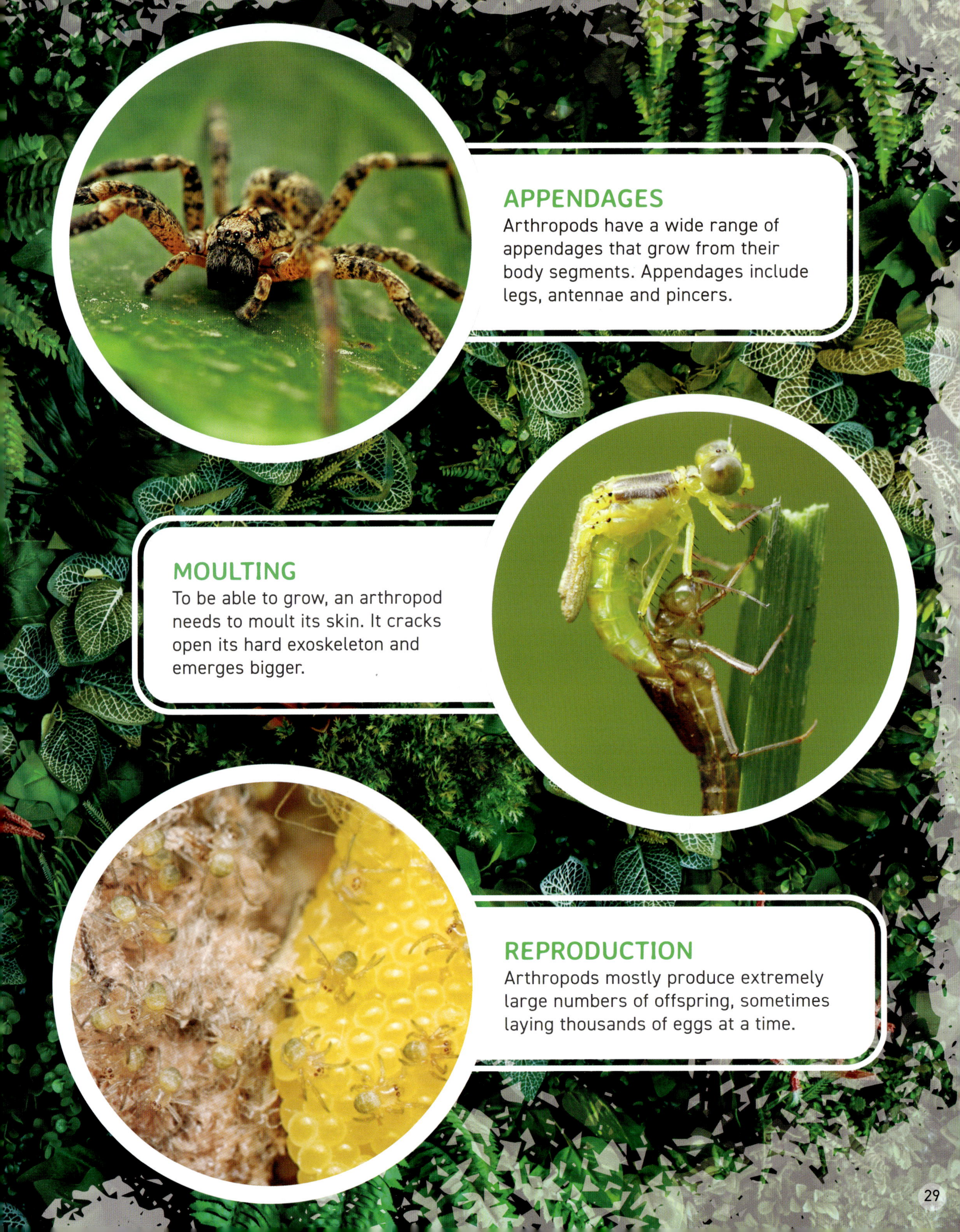

## APPENDAGES

Arthropods have a wide range of appendages that grow from their body segments. Appendages include legs, antennae and pincers.

## MOULTING

To be able to grow, an arthropod needs to moult its skin. It cracks open its hard exoskeleton and emerges bigger.

## REPRODUCTION

Arthropods mostly produce extremely large numbers of offspring, sometimes laying thousands of eggs at a time.

# ALIEN LIFE

**Arthropods look so weird up close that we can easily imagine them as creatures from outer space. This is not an entirely foolish idea!**

## EXOSKELETONS

Some scientists believe that intelligent life in other galaxies and solar systems could be similar to arthropods in a number of ways. Alien life might have an external skeleton, instead of internal bones like humans do.

## DELICATE FINGERS

They might also have limbs with extensions such as those that insects and spiders have. These specialised fingers would be able to perform very delicate tasks, such as designing and making a spaceship.

## SPACE TRAVEL

A hard, outer skeleton would be useful in helping life forms travel through space and withstand conditions that would destroy a body with soft skin.

# GLOSSARY

**abdomen** body part at the rear of an arthropod

**carnivore** animals that eats mostly meat

**evolve** change over time to adapt to a habitat

**exoskeleton** hard, outer covering of an arthropod

**mandible** sharp jaws of an arthropod

**omnivore** animal that eats both plants and meat

**phylum** one of the major groups of living things

**pincer** sharp body part that grabs tightly

**sac** small bag created by a living thing to hold liquids or eggs

**thorax** middle body part of an arthropod

**wingspan** width of both wings

# INDEX